The Bed of Memory

for Ted

Jean Earle

The Bed of Memory

seren

seren
is the book imprint of
Poetry Wales Press Ltd
Nolton Street, Bridgend, Wales
www.seren-books.com

ISBN 1-85411-295-3

A CIP record for this title is available from
the British Library

*The publisher works with the financial assistance of the
Arts Council of Wales*

Cover Image: detail from 'Cyn Elo'r Haul' by Elin Huws
(wool, mohair, cotton, silk, on mohair warp)

Printed in Palatino by
Bell & Bain Ltd, Glasgow

Contents

The Pink Handkerchief

As a handkerchief, fallen on a lawn,
Floats up its cry of pink
From surrounding green –
So colours charge me now, urgent and fresh
Beyond what age expects.

Ripple your flags, you enhanced frequencies
And say what you mean – warning or gift?
For it must be something is happening?

When I was young such splendid projections
Told me my name. A gift, certainly....
Life began from then. But what is this,
Now that the colours leap at me anew?
Another spring?

And yet – a thing my mother used to tell
Of her father, dying; how his faded eyes
At the moment of truth
Turned the bluest blue?

The Old Believers

Changes in Godspeak fused them
Into rocks; shifting across
Landslides of schism until they piled
At extremity of cold; where glittering trees
Vandyke forever
On and on; to the Sea of Japan.

They were God's geology, its fossil flowers,
The Old Believers.

Three hundred years
No hunter hunted them.
They were the hunters. They took bear,
Wolf, wolverine; and wore their Faith
Like radiant furs, constant about them.

A plough in common,
A few farm animals....
The ghostly summers
Breathed up from permafrost:
Fungi and berries, stars of water,
Their thin crops.

They thanked their God who had backpacked
With them, offering no favours. The unchanged Word,
Simple as cold,
Was all their trade – the Old Believers.

Each man his hut
In the forest, his roaring stove
Against mortality; silence and distance

To chop and trap. Even the children
Honed a stone pride. Sometimes the elders,
Tired, wandered the night woods,

Seeking God; finally stunned by Him
Between the moonlit stripes
And the mauve shadows. So they lived and died.
Perverse.

They were the Old Believers.

The Extra Eye

One day, when I was young, an inner eye
Opened to help the shy dark-blue eyes
I was born with. Something I had read
Or thought or suffered sprang this extra aid
To assessing the world. It was for looking.

Looking is other than seeing.

A Spring day; and this accessory
Suddenly evolved. Did I always know
Or had, until then, been dead?
As a huge Indian jewel
Differs from a grit, it clarified
Patterns and geometries
Striping the whole of life. Immense tides of land
As well as waves of the sea; Vibrations of mind
Matching the pulses of stars. Empathy of leaves
One to another with the shudderings of grass
Roughly shorn; root-shrieks of weeds,
Sheens between animal fur and the fuzz
On the backs of bees....

And the personal light flowing from ourselves,
Glowing with us from birth – and, shortly before death,
Leaving us. Extinguished? Or to ignite
Undreamed of insights which even the extra eye
Cannot contain? I looked and looked at the world,
Was comforted. And laughed.

As the Irishman said
Of Communion bread changing into flesh,
"Why wouldn't it?"

The Blue Corridor

Remember resting bones
In the afternoons?

Dreaming along the walls
Of a blue corridor – that curved away
Like a swan's neck. All doors open
So that power welled softly
Out from the rooms, playing across
Worn, bumpy plaster until a skylight
Hurled full sun down among the blues.

Always the rested mind
Turns home; as when a child
Steals from play to catch the mother's skirt.
Clings. Runs on....

Whether we painted over
Or let stains fade. Nevertheless,
Raging electrics shimmer the blue corridor,
Memory. My arm glows
Along your radiant spine. Asleep together,
We were a closed circuit, generating
Birth, love, death – all that it means, to live.

The fields of force!
The colours!

Mimes of ourselves
Ripple from doorways, towards the curve.
We, those before
And to come after us....

This is an old house.
The skylight rays down hard
Into the changing blues,
Blinding the years.

The Guillemot

Full tide now
In the afternoons.
Through this round of green glass
A young guillemot dives,
Coming up farther off
By the cliff's white frill.
At such distance we cannot tell
Whether it has a fish?

No money and no goods....
Only inherited zest,
The beak always a gleam ahead.
Perhaps a fish.
Perhaps not.

Its shadow distorts
As it trails down. Now it loses
This life-companion, over darker sand
And a black causeway
Hidden beneath.
Its shining curve
Surfaces again – oh, look!
The shadow has caught a fish.

Working up to light
From cold depths –
Beak and feet aligned
With the need to hunt, to feed,
To live....
Always within the wet-suit's
Limiting shape; which it cannot change
Because it fits the life.
A fish, at any rate for this tide....
We know the feeling well!

By the Pond

The heron never trusted me but rose
At my footfall, all my life, till now.

Hunched by the pond
In a mood of invisibility,
Rigid with my concerns (as the heron is
With his) he suddenly swooped behind me,
Cracking the staves of his wings
Loose and loud, an inch from my head.

His trailed legs
Caught up the shadow of my accidie
Into the natural world – his home tree,
Rocking with light and air....

And I was free.

A Grave at Aldburgh

The other night,
In a late slot (for the minority),
Peter Pears returned. A tall figure,
Clothed for storm, he sang for me alone
"Die Winterreise".

I wanted to ask him –
Granted his gift and a velvet listener –
How he could probe so deep into my world
(Which was not his) as to stir romance
In an old person sitting in her night-dress?
He wandered the Moor,
Haunted by the Crow; followed the lovely curves
Of the Stream and the Linden tree – past her gate
That would never open to him. Passion and sadness
Darkened his voice with such integrity....

Yet he is long gone
Under the earth; lying beside
Another man. Not far off,
The waves mutter and mouth
On that cold shore. Of such tides, too, he once
Was *meister-singer* and interpreter.

Porth-y-Rhaw

I was here before....
What I remember is a giant's comb
Rusting in the grass. Between its teeth
Rags of wool whipped in the wind.
"An old loom", said the voice
Holding my hand.

It is an April evening
After a warm day. Still.
A path humps and greens
Above the lute of a stream
Glittering on
Through a dry scent of earth.

The path falls suddenly,
Into a raging cove
Shocked with high tide. Here, long ago,
Somebody (who?) swam and hurt himself
Against dark rocks?

The voice explaining the loom
Is dead – and I,
Stung by the spray,
Watch a hawk which scarcely quivers
In the dusking sky.

A Bush of Stars

Overlooking the sink,
A star of Bethlehem bush.

We work darkened by its presence.
"Oh, put on the light..."
And last out winter days, irked
By the clump of tossed, sighing skeletons.

But in July – you should see us then!
Stars for our hair, the very taps entwined
With yellow trespassers, hundreds of joys.
A leaf scents the pinch
With delicate oil. Flowers press high
Off the balmy person of this bush
With an authority – such as fine speakers ray
From a stage or festival bells peal.

After summer storms, stem shadows
Jig chandelier repeats on the kitchen wall.
But when the night seems long....
We know the bush is part
of all we do not go out into,
Under harder stars,
Glinting a dark of which we are afraid.

Before bedtime, when domestic glare
Reflects last moves in the window pane,
I see my hands washing up in the bush.
Taps gush through the flowers, steam wavers
Spirit-like – as it were, myself
Working from a hide. Of course it is the glass does this
By magic. Yet I love to feel
I am part of the bush. Translated thus,
May I not lift a front to those other stars
And still be safely
Rinsing a dish?

The Catalyst

Dusk; and a mad wind. She went out
To the log-pile and saw fire
Raging up the coast, flicking inland
Wild as a bird on scarlet wings.

The man she had lately married was down a cleft
Of the grazing, doctoring sheep. For the first time,
She shouted his name. It left her throat
Rough, unaccustomed; was lost on the wind.

Since he had picked her out
From among the convict-factory's bad girls,
They had come clumsily together, got through chores,
Managed without names. A taciturn man....
She had been a number and had half forgotten
How she used to be called.
They were, in most ways, strangers. He said little,
Whether she slept with him or on the beach,
Finding herself once more, cleansing her past
In the big swells, curling among plants
With bitter seeds and pricks,
Above sand and stones. But now, she shrieked his name
And he did not hear. She ran back
To the fowl house and shooed out the hens
In a helpless gesture. The fire gained fast.
Through smoke, out of the whining grass
Rose flies and moths and bats – the cabin fence
And her dress were tacked with gems of their eyes.

At last, he came – blackened and scorched –
And crying. She had not dreamed
The silent man could cry? "The flock was gone
And the dog, in a flash takeover..." He had loved the dog,
She knew. He was driving two sheep

Somehow before him. She urged him down
A defile, to the shore – and there they penned the sheep
In a niche of rock and huddled there themselves,
Hearing the fire licking the bluff above,
Crackling the cabin, with a cough smell
Of burn, feathers and desolation. Along the shore
Night fell. The long tide went out. Now and again, a star
Sparkled in a pool. She scooped water,
Laving his burns with salt. Such a dreary peace
Quietened the land above, the fire past.

He kept on saying, "How shall we live?" And she,
So long excluded from anyone's thoughts
For the future, had no answer – did what came
More natural to her now. She spoke his name.

Dorothy Wordsworth

I

(Before William's marriage)

Walking — as scissors open and shut,
Mechanical, intent — miles against the wind,
For his letter.

He said he would not marry? Since he's away,
These headaches come. My head will break....
Not the head. The heart.

How happy we have been....
Planting the scarlet beans,
Tramping the hills. At our deepest accord
He goes for Mary?

He does as he must. His prudent plans
Include me. He never left me out
Of childhood games.

I had not shared my Self
Ever before; nor roamed the starry night.
We had become a single Stargazer.

II

Not well, today. Gathered the scarlet beans.
Washed my head. Put up sheets.
Wrote to Mary....

III

Always I kept for him
Things he might lose. All night I wore his ring,
He gave it me again, and with a look,
Blessed me. The strangeness of this day
Founders me. I must lie down....

IV

(*After William's marriage*)

What is it that she has
And I have not? A kinder fate....
She is not his sister.

Before we three made one
He immortalised me
In a homage of verse. "The shooting lights
Of thy wild eyes...."
She tends the fire
Behind the words. She does what I do not.
She is his bed, table, chair. We are dark and light,
Forging the ring we both must wear
To band his mind's tower.

V

They shut the door. I never dream his dreams
Now, in my sleep — but, like a mother,
Suddenly wake, hearing his children cry.

Light snow today. Paper my new room
With old news. Write out Ariosto.
Make a rabbit pie.

VI

(*Dorothy in later years*)

Beside the lake today, a Rock
Brilliant with moss! Once, I might have set
This emerald into William's writing hand.
No more. I am old before my time and strange,
Strange. I tear my hat in rage. My mind sees
Emerald to light the world – yet my tongue spills
Nonsense and fret. I am wheeled about the place
By William's child.

The Palace Office

Long brown room, fluent with shadows.
Letters, columns of tots; the poems flushing and fading
Between efficiencies.
Flickered sun on hollies, some holy battle
Of light and dark, in whatever season.
Wildness at tall windows –
Creaking heron; or buzzard
Mewing, high above copier, telephone, files.
Sometimes, the Bishop's
Quick visitation. Work, and a kind word.
"The spotted flycatcher has arrived!" And there,
An arm-length from my typewriter, the bird from Africa!

Over the years this room had other uses,
from storing apples to country dance –
Traditional jigs
Lumped by the village girls. (No boys.)

Earlier, another Bishop sat
Watching his fancy geese cackle and feed
On wintry lawns. Shawled against chill,
He wrote his thoughts to a young girl.
"Letters to a Friend", a minor classic.
"So cold in my great house
I dread going to bed."

It was a warm room
In my time. Squirrels at the sills,
An afterthought fox – and once, a snake,
Thirsting for water, glided among us
In hot weather. I helped it out,
Looped on a deft umbrella. My colleagues shuddered,
Fled to another room – but I,
I felt privileged.

And once, some outworn robes were left
In the hall, for disposal – and I (no harm)
With office scissors cut a stealthy swath
For a petticoat. Such firm black satin
Where it wasn't subtly moused
Or holed by moth. It almost stood alone
And was hard to sew. No one ever knew
What I wore sometimes beneath my office skirt
When I took dictation.

As it Was Then

An afternoon street of miners' houses.
He and she, in love and despair,
Climbing towards her house on the mountain.

Her arms full of bluebells. The young man,
Bemused and guilty, troubled
After their quarrel in the woods.
Housewives in caps and aprons
Gape and fall silent. Perhaps they knew
Bluebells once – but their lives have long
Hardworked them out of mind. He and she,
Flushed and angry, hurry from ordeal of eyes
To her house on the mountain.

The bluebells greying already; asking only
A looser clutch, connection with the earth,
Water.

The Cucumber Frame

His trowel tried the soil
Of the cucumber frame. We noticed the ants'
Display of eggs – military beadwork
Warming to life under the glass cover.

"Huh!" he said, going off to boil water.

But at the trowel's thrust,
The ants began hiding their eggs away,
In perfect drill. Soon there was no sign
Of their next generation. All disappeared
Under a light camouflage of earth.

I remembered myself –
Running from bombs,
A young, hysterical woman, Patsy and Paul
Clutched to my breast, dangling small legs,
Falling into the shelter. Not like the ants'
Elegant withdrawal. Surely these creatures *know*
Beyond instinct, what they are about?

I felt respect – and hope –
For their disciplined manoeuvre,
As though I understood their world –
Other than ours; yet linked by some alert
Between differences?

It was a new sensation,
Almost of belonging. Why do we never think
Of ants and men as refugees together
From like situations?

Then came the cucumber grower
With his boiling water.

On Reading Proust

Buddings of innuendo
Open to slow and careful reading

As a bee meticulously visits
Every stigma in a fertile patch,
Learning the intimate pollens
Of each one.

So I learned you
Through our long closeness,
The rich years teaching us, offering honeys,
Enigmas. I came to know you
Deeply; yet not at all. Trying the world
Hand in hand
Or lying cold in bed...
Where sometimes I might find myself to be
Wholly woman and not man's woman
As one needs to be
For a strong coming together....

I would assume, like Proust,
The very art of mood. For hours I stared
Into the dark, probing what it is to be
One; or two; or fused... until I could not bear
The turning inside-out of human deeps –
Proust-wise. A fraught spell
In that beady-eyed loneliness and I turned
Into your arms.

Old Photographs

You, me, they,
With ordered smiles....
Just-married or at some other wedding,
Firmly hatted and not ourselves....

One not born until after such photographs
Turns the smiles over.
Auntie's face, Grandpa's, yours or mine.

I remember a sunny verandah
Trellised with roses, the kind that smell
Like washing on the line.
Where the sun centred, glass-framed negatives
Developing the smiles – that hid what else
Of darkness? – yet here's one
Rinsed in the bathroom basin (window screened,
No one to need the loo
Till the magic had worked) their murky promise
Sharpening as they swirled in the bowl.

An old camera's evidence
How two parted, lost their smiles, appeared
In the album again, after the heat and glare
And rinsings of life. Through the time-foxed pages
Here they recur – hopeful, scowling,
One without the other. Then, at last,
Seated closely, at a great age,
Smiling.

Of a Long Ago Death

When you had just died....
In the dumbfounded silence of the room
I cried out,
"Where have you gone?"

The years since then,
The happenings!
Children you never saw,
Their children....
The good husbands and homes....

Supposing you came back
To receive this news,
How the family tongues
Would run and run!

In our excitement, might we forget to ask
"Where have you been?"

Having That

Under huge clouds of may.
The children running before,
Breakfast in their hands....
While past our cheeks and hair
Floated those shining threads
Whereby certain spiders voyage the sunlit air
To suitable nesting sites.

We have had that.

Newly married,
Walking a moonlit shore.
The incoming waves
Suddenly phosphorescent
Peacock and silver,
So that we clung to each other
Stared at the wild glory.

We have had that.

Life — looking back — was a heap of leaves
In a private wood
Which we inhabited,
Burying nuts like squirrels.
Digging them out,
Savouring, marvelling....
Clinging to each other
Over the bitter ones. Spit out —
Tremble. Forget.... On to the next eccentricity.

Till our teeth cracked. Then we went in
From the wood and made a softer bed
Where you would drowsily ask,
"What time is it?" And I would say,
"Time for another little sleep...."
So we would nap again,
Warmly together.

We have had that.

A Day Away

After grief....
The hurt became too sore
For obsessive touching of such pain....

Do not touch. In another dimension
Repeat some jaunt when you were easy together,
Neither unbearably happy nor trying to find
Solutions. Perhaps an outing taken
Many times before?

On a summer morning. Off on a train,
The country quiet after hay. Willowherb
Flaring the tracks so that you cry
"Look at that!" But he, up early,
Is stealing a little nap against your shoulder.

When you arrive – that side shop
Where you've bought chocolate and fruit
Time and again. Standing to smell the sea,
Putting your feet in the water. Later on,
Down to the quay and stuck there, watching boats,
Dizzy with sunshine. Up round the hill
To your known bench facing the Bay.
Eating your picnic – remnants to that gull
With the twisted claw, an old friend.
Silently brooding the sea's
Blues and greens as though the turning day
Were yours forever – then, at the crown of the hill,
Spreading your coats between a scatter of strangers,
Lounging on grass and drowsing away
The afternoon – sometimes aware
Of the westering sky and the tide's changing tune.

Drifting, at last, gently towards the town
And familiar café. Plaice-and-chips,
Bread-and-butter and tea. It is cool now,
The road to the station gauzed with mist
As in dreams. And the train home
Rollicky, rollicky, taking its time.

And once home — though it is barely dark,
Climbing to bed so slowed, so sweet with sun
You can scarcely move. As though
Too tired to touch the grief, falling asleep
With the past; but now,
Though only one in the bed,
Closer than ever.

In Hospital

How shall we last this winter out?
Nourishment
Tossed us at random by a hope
Hovering always in the pleat of storm,
Brighting short blues
Between mountains, as a bird
Flying crosswind (a sudden space
And a drop). Rigours of the beloved
Who is in death's shadow.

After a visit, going to bed
Alone. Then, after wakeful hours,
Sun flaming the window bars
With diamond; like a wonderful smile
After misunderstanding.

So this winter is, in stripes of smile
And shadow. Hurrying corridors,
Climbing stairs, producing smiles,
Smiles.... And home to something hot,
Contact with an animal. The face wet
Without knowing it. Falling asleep
Again – again –
Against a hard place.

To Vera's

Faceless Vera....
Your ambience, somehow
The colour of plums.

Your room.
My mother drawing me up
Endless stairs. *My little legs, Vera....*
The sudden light. Laughter and tears
Ricocheted off walls.

Tongues of reproach, ley-lines,
Crimes of the dead. How did I know this,
Having no language but my needs?
By the tenderly stroked,
Bitterly pricked fur of their tones.

Your bed, Vera....
Deep, white. I trampolined
Till I was tired.

Then – the chocolate,
(Always just one, huge)
Jelled up my mouth
With rapturous gloy. Who *was* Vera?
Ought I to remember
Any of those people?

Bounce; and bounce, bounce,
At the tall window
Mad with light. A bird
Floated between myself and cars
Miles below.

Vera, with no face, plum-soft,
Plum-rich. Your wound
That I had no word for? All these years
I have recalled – each feather plain –
The back of the bird.

A Goodbye

How magical the world has been,
Shimmering and remarkable....

And to have gone through life
With one more practical, less achingly susceptible
Than oneself – yet perfectly open
To being shown marvels. His eye would widen,
Smiling upon the news – and understand.

What bliss that was, to be privileged to share
Marvels – with one who participated
Not as though analysing dreams
Or dividing a fruit,
But as the natural flow
Of one river into another stream.
Sunset infusing amethyst
Across the confluence....

Seeing whatever it was
Not dazzled through my eyes
But as though making them
Stronger to bear this cross
Of sometimes unmanageable grace.

A Back Road

This heap of stones was a house
Of one night, that grandfather threw up
In his youth; with a morning smoke
And a boiled kettle; then worked on a barn
And a place for sleep. Up a ladder
To a half-top, his son was born,
Tom (or John?) Who later had two boys,
Dick and Will. They played here
Where the churn stood, scrawling boys' dirty things
With bits of slate on the slate stand.

Dick's wife – what happened to her? An old man knows
She had a singing voice as she milked
Or scratched in the yard: but it was heard
Seldom. She is long gone.
Where? People forget
So much. And this is a back road.

Spring simmers and burns. On the warm slab
Of the churn stand an adder suns. He is no harm
To anyone, if left alone.
In his stillness. This is his place now.
The lorry comes no more
To frighten him off. This is a back road.

The Oxford Book of English Verse

(*i.m. Gwen*)

We were not touching or kissing friends.
More like boys in our hard links
With each other – that never broke....
Sometimes running aground
For a while or, in satirical letters,
Keeping the shine on steel. At last –
Cruelly aged from the girls we were –
Catching the instantly recognised,
Casual hail of your now solitary
Life to mine. Robust chats
On the telephone, keeping it light....

Tonight, I sit with a book you gave me
Seventy years ago; your dark eyes
Mocking my choice. "*Poetry?*"
You'll never ring
Again with your half-amused,
Understated loneliness. I touch the ghost
Of your young hand – dashing with the pen
As with youth and life –
Writing my name.

Night and Day

Our garden ghosts with Himalayan balsam,
Far more beautiful
Than the park flowers we used to grow
When we were active and entire.
These propagate themselves like giant orchids
From addictive pinching of their pods. Time after time,
Drifting outside to check the rising moon,
My mischievous old hand springs off the seeds.

Surfaces get fuzzier. Day by day
I dust – but especially under our bed
Fluff-balls gather – which are beautiful too,
In the eye's beholding. If we had the will
To set up the microscope, what revelations
Would astound me! Dust is a marvel
When you consider it. And I do.

So old now.... we sleep like animals,
Where we flop. Food is whenever
The body says it's fainting. I stand,
With my night cramps, flexing my hands and feet
By moonlight. The Himalayan balsam
Gleams its ethereal silks. There is a heady smell
Of earth. The cramps are painful
But it helps to bend joints, the moon shining so hard
And the world turning, mystical through the night,
Sweating grass and flowers....

Rhondda Pilgrimage

When we went back to see what had happened
After forty years — I was afraid to look
From the pub window. But Pen Pych
Soared almost from the bar, drifting its belts
Of white cloud.

Changes there were, big changes — though rain poured,
Familiar. Stonecrop along walls
Sunned the dark copings. That and Pen Pych
Used to be our markers on grimy mornings,
Running for the train....
For we had to deny that dead end,
Grasp at chance, desperately snatch
What might help us escape....

Yet we loved the place. Never imagined
Women in the pubs, green games
Where the pit was, a different myth
Trivialising the Valley face.

So it is, when you go back and look....
No one left (you were so long gone).
Constants of landscape stand
For human ghosts. Pen Pych; and the brilliant weed
Married to the stone.

Salt

Some tears are salt beyond
Seasoning of grief. We relate to salt.
When bad things happen
It becomes addictive. We taste ourselves
Through crises – as the natural world
Sweats saltish essences, inherent skills
Against storm and drought.
The green suffering and pains of flesh
Different yet linked; related
Like brothers and sisters.

Sample this spring leaf – sweet yet salt –
Or the winter bark of its tree, sour-fresh

And vaguely salt
Which is the universal
Condiment and sting.

Too much is not good for us.
We try to limit the sift
Over the lonely meals, iced walkways,
Self-indulgent fears....
On innermost hurts we weep our saltiness
Unrestrained, to unblock
Mortal dryness
As do parched roots and courageous flowers.

Do you not feel the power of salt
Infusing everything? Mingling human tears
And green exhalations,
A symbiosis? Surely the grass lies down
Under a black wind as we lie too,
Salting our sorrows. And the sea's salt
Tangs of our origins and chains of time.
For we come from the sea.

A Cry

My love, help me!

You, who came to believe
After death, there is nothing but the dark....

A reasonable, just and scientific conclusion,
(You said) after a full life.

We argued it out,
Your honesty tenderly constraining me
Who would will happy immortality
Both on ourselves and every thing that lives
And shines and dies without our human need
To imagine God....

Out of the charged silence in which you left me,
My love, help me!

Bereavement

Sunlight an insult still,
Darkness a hiding place....

Music; the family's new-born,
Other deaths...
Experienced from far off.

I forced myself to make bread,
Cold hands warming to the dough
Deeper, stronger,
As to some primitive instruction....

And then they suddenly found themselves
Out in the air, cutting flowers
To look at through tears.

Do not feel that you betray
The unbreakable link by answering such calls.
Eat a little, meddle at something simple
And old as time. It will show you death
As though sorrow
Can, in the end, take a form of birth.

Going Home

Across the cliff as we flagged homeward
After a hot day,
The sun swelled west, staining its juice
Over a parched and dry earth.
The sea shone bloody. Sweeps of grasses
Reddened far off. The white campions
Stared up pink. I saw you
Standing ahead, transfigured — a bronze man
Flaring an aura in the haze. A prince....

I thought, "It will never be like this again...."
And it never was.

Two Years

We were born about the same time.
Now I am two years older than you.

Two years (they encourage me) is the normal span
Before life can restart. I only want to feel
Our native air on our young faces....
Wind in the fern
That smelled of the sea. You running with me
Over the mountain; and the sunlight sweeping
Huge shadows, we rushing out of them,
Laughing. Your warm hands
Holding me. We kiss for the first time
Under that rainy tree.

Not as young lovers of today,
Locked together in a crowded street,
Knowing it all — but as it was then,
Shy and amazed. The other day
They took me — not laughing or leaping now
But in a car — to look for the tree
That put down roots
Long before ours. It stands as it did
And still the rain sings through
Its eloquent leaves
That, for my help, renewed
Old-fashioned Spring.

And I needed you....

The Surprise

When we were very old,
Lying in bed one night, I dreamed of us
When young. And, suddenly,
I was hipped with rainbows
Circling, sparkling, up and around the flesh
Of a sweet woman.

The last such experience and the very best
Of our long span
Together. But it was only myself....
You never knew of it,
Sleeping in the dark as free of me
As though you were dead?

How, without urge, you ravished me
Silently; making no move in the bed
And nothing said.

Frustrations of Creation

She sends her selves
Out from herself....

Seated among plants that grow towards her,
Thirsty. She is made of light
Absorbed from their growing, offered back
In rhythms and water

She grows with their growing. Light enters her
Also from the sky — a startling —
And strikes, blinding, into hand and pen.
Light she returns is not of such quality
As she receives — the smite of it diffused
Among objects of day crowding around her,
Selves may flit from her at any time.
She is container of all — and they are many.
All will return.
Often at night, she deals them out
Like a pack of cards, one here, one there,
To be looked over, changed about,
Perhaps not used
After all, in creation's fever.

She laughs in the dark with lovers,
Becomes a trapped moth — or dreams
Endless manifestations like persicaria
Which no gardener
Applauds, standing up stiff
Inadequate corals, on infertile ground.

Out go the selves, hopeful,
One by one, till she lies alone,
Empty. All around, the plants wait for light.
One of them is the piece of a flower

Eaten away by slugs, lingering in a cup
She found for it; blazing distorted scraps
Of a wonderful red.
All her potential concentrates through it
Into the cracked cup – that holds
Eerily bright water.

The Way it Goes

After you died, my love, in devastation
I said to you, "I'll come as soon as I can...."
Truly convinced I would follow you
Almost at once – perhaps in hours.

I soon learned the body won't let go
Until its time, no matter how the grief
Wills to an end. Before long
(To the grief's horror) the flesh shouts "Food!"
And, when denied, bothers for this and that
It fancies in particular,
Till, like an itch
That must be scratched, it eats

Even for two.
And next, one day it notices the warmth
On its own side of the marital bed –
Or how the martins have returned
To the stricken house
Or how the light
Blazes those twigs when you glance, half-blind
From your would-be dying.

After a while,
However the spirit mourns
The face stops crying.

Two Women

She who lives opposite
Can never be my friend. She goes to the shop
In her black chador. We are often there
Together, with our fancies. She has this yen
For oranges. My craving's cheese.
I nibble as I pay. She must hold out
Till he who minds her everywhere
Shepherds her home, wordless.
She has none of our words.
And I have none of hers. Yet here we are,
Two women, almost ripe. The black chador
Covers her well – but I am wise to
Her lonely pregnancy. I feel her eyes
Estimate my belly and my bold greed
For cheese. As she sways out
Behind the man, her oranges burn
Against the blackness draping long and full
About her other fruit. *What's in there*?

They are home. The man shuts the door.
Nothing can be done.
At dusk, to cheer my singleness, I switch on
The bright paper globe – that leaps its shape
Beyond the window, three repeats of light
From here to there. One lands –
The wishful gift of an orange –
On her step.

The Ritual Meals

Feed!
Cattle on green, man on flesh
And grains that swell to full,
Consuming the dark earth

Creatures invisibly small
Colonise your blonde lashes
My beautiful love –
Your brows.

Who would imagine it!
They feed on ichors
From the clear iris,
On lamp-shaped tears.

Perhaps the dead feed
On our memories of them? Themselves host
To swarms of transforming force
And ravening beauty.

God, then? How does He feed – upon us?
I see His huge, fierce face
Sweeping the naked souls
As they leave their bones.

His mouth widens. They filter through
Scarves of exquisite light, auroras....
Where to? Nobody knows.

Behind the Left Shoulder

I have asked others
(Risking their speculative stare
At my sanity) whether they, too,
Are attuned to "angels"? To my surprise,
Several confess to having one in tow
Coming or going with a need. "Why, yes –
I'm often conscious of *something there....*"

A half-forgotten child
Crouched on the lawn while clover flowers
Darkened in the grass.
A smell of ironing coming from the house –
And overhead, the moon,
Pondered for the first time.

An angel is not a peculiarity
One talks of lightly
Or boastingly. A curious appendage,
Delicate, strange....
And perhaps not an angel at all
But a familiar? All my life,
Positioned so that, if I turn my head
I am aware of a small moon
Constant behind my left shoulder.
Mostly, I forget...

Somehow connected with being alone
Outside, at the coming of night.
Consolation against
What may happen and what has been
And the tears from that.

The Dressing Gown

For my birthday.... But why a thing
So expensively beautiful?
When we are old
We sometimes ponder (oddly shrewd and cold)
On those we deeply love. She is our family flesh,
Our tender touch, our irritant delight.

Remember her as a child, prancing barefoot
Across iced pools, on a Christmas walk?
She was never cold, she took no chill
From her dancing, always had it all –
The shared cake and the whole; and would give away
Careless, reckless, her last chance.

It hangs behind my door, a waterfall
Gleaming in the night. It draws the dawn
When I cannot sleep. A ray from the car park
Wanders a ruby over the satin folds,
Where I lie, wakeful, pondering. Was it a gift from one
She no longer sees? And so she passed it on?
Deft with the frost and sunshine
Whatever she paid....
Nothing? Or more than she could afford?

Bless her! May she always command
Satin surprises – and skip warm
Across ice, keeping us all at bay
Who mistrust (yet smile at) her gifts...
And never come to harm
Whatever she spend.

A Missed Migration

Last week, the martins left,
Leaving a chick
In the nest. Its white cheek-flash
Gaped from the ragged cup
A day – then hung.
At any time,
In and out of the house,
I know it to be there.
Not the death I mind –
But life's failure
To shoot this arrow
Off its miraculous bowstring
To the bulls-eye sun.

1947

Snow fell....
Fell and fell. Froze.
Birds died,
Darkly dotting the high white roads
Redwing, fieldfare, starling
Scattered inert.

A robin came into the kitchen
And lived in a basket.

Sometimes I stood
With the child inside me, to use in her making
Sheaves and veils of aurora
Shifting between the stars.
"Look..." I'd say, silently
Showing her through my eyes.

Across buried fields
People clumped miles, for bread.
A ship brought flour
Into the haven. All the gulls
Wasted inland; the very foam
Froze. We skidded and slid
To the well — that lightly steamed
Under its cap of snow, sequinned
By fugitive sun. A fern lived on
In a sealed spring, an iced dome
Of clearest glass, lasting the cruel months
On and on.

I curled about
Her forming self, under many quilts.
They brought the kettle
Hot to my bed, from a hoarded fire.

We tell it still....
And now my daughter, then unborn,
Ushers her summer grandchildren
In at the door where the robin's basket
Hung — where I stood out
Breathing the frost, showing her hidden armature
The Northern Lights.

For Lib's and Ned's New Boy

What is it like, your first day
Out in the world? The firm shawl
Binds you, harsher than the float
Of the womb. This new thing – air –
Opens and shuts the frail web
Of your breath. Bright sounds
Invade your ear, faces and lights confuse
Your tender sight. Sleep's the best cover-all
now you have left
The fierce protective round of your mother.
(And your father wept
At your miracle, your mother's pain.)

As yet you have no dreams.
Growth will bring dreams. May they be such
As young gods move in, full of noble colours,
Cliffs where you never fall and wild creatures
Safe by your authority. May life and death
Be glorious for you. If, in some strong
Experience of the dark, nightmares should come –
Love always be in the next room for you!

On Some Loss of Hearing

When I was younger, I could hear the sea
From a field away. Now
I must go to the sands. The same with birds
In a nearby wood – and the high, silver say
Of grandchildren. My ears are old.

I miss eavesdropping
In the Beach Café – my hearing then
A bat's for verity.
Changeable as the sea
Drifted towards me surgings from other lives,
Grits and currents....
Now and again a Pearl (perfectly safe with me).

Oh, from tables and tables away....

Remembering Mrs Morgan

When a brief revenant
Slips inexplicably into that warm dusk
Where you cherish your dead,
Saying, "Remember me?"

Remember her.

Out of haze, bring to a sharp edge
What you knew of her. Perhaps as a child,
Noting red hands and a smell of milk.
In later encounters, thinking how small her bosom was
After many pregnancies. Meeting once
In rain, she suddenly told
Of the phantom funeral that left her house
Before he died. You recollect
The sun came out as she spoke
And beamed so strong
On her faith in the sighting – which you had not.

Another age....
to which, by long life and memory
You are slightly connected. She has a right
To your difficult recall.

Remember her.

Where We are When We are Not Here

Instant transition
From whatever's happening
To the random footprints
Of time gone....

Diverting from the apex of love even
To so small a scene; perhaps no more
Than the rough brown towels a lover liked,
Strewing the wet floor
On a summer night

Or, without warning,
Drifting some intimately known
Inflow of sea, sunlit — your shadow under you
Private as a bird flying.

So, also, the gnarled griefs
Once inhabited
Leer upon us suddenly,
Trailing remembered furnishings,
Streets, weather....
Fouling the very springs of joy.
Mostly though, sources of consolation....
Coming to mind
As the quiet bed will or the worn,
Comfortable shoe. Where I am
When I am not here....

It is always sunset
Behind hills. Sheep gather,
Carrying on their fleece
Soft blooms of light.

Bad Dreams

I and my mother
Looking, after rain, at the bright drops on the bushes....
Comradely; as though two queens admired
Jewels that their beautiful children would inherit.

My father had not come home – who for days
had brooded
A familiar darkness. She said to me
(Woman to woman, not mother to daughter)
"You know, if it were all to be
Over again, I would have no one but him...."

Then I dreamed he came home
To that shadowy room he inhabited. Although so young,
I sensed what clouded him. I cried.
"You are thin and cold...." and put my arms around
(As I never did) to comfort him.
"She says, if it were to be
Over again, she would have no one but you...."
"Ah. Did she say that with her voice?"

Yes, father, with her voice. Here was the heart of it –
What she told me in dream was true....
Though in waking life she would never have said so.
This was the eye of my father's
Meagre and bitter weather.
Yet, in an odd way, they belonged to each other?

Worse. Outside a dream
I and my mother would never have shared
The shining after rain. Nor could my father's
Pride have allowed a perceptive child
To understand his pain.

Looking at the Sea

My guardian angel nudges me.
"Shift yourself, make an effort, move
Your slow legs, your negative will,
And look at the sea!"

Echoing sky, obsessively speaking its name
Against the shore, tilting the rafts of gulls
At their foraging. Up and down
Like a lullaby. "Come...."

"Stir your stumps, you old and tired lover –
You may never look at the sea again. "

Never again? But the stones turn rhythmically over
Tides of the past. Something there is....
When we are gone, of what gave pleasure
In the wash of pain. One who comes after,
Wearing my print, will also hear the sea
Remembering itself. White birds
And serene blue where the stiffening feet
Enjoyed the water. Breathing deep
As a swimmer,
Ray outward that last look.

Breathing Exercises

I breathe again
Up through the vitals and the belly-button....
Air that just resembles sanity
After that almost mortal blow you dealt me.

I fell over.
All the breath went out of me;
Weak with the long anguish it comes back....
Not the breathing it was
When our lives lifted and subsided
In unison. Now it is a doctor's prescription,
Sufficient for the day.

I think of your last words to me –
"Eat plenty. Mind those stairs."
The tail end of a marriage...
And I fall over again.

Restored but lesser breath affects my seeing
So that I seem to notice smaller things –
Wonders, delicates, intricates – that there was not time
To notice before.

As when a student tries new spectacles
And views his future study differently,
With deeper vision of the way
To tackle it in future. Breathe up and out,
Away from your death....

Not away from you, not you...
But from pain I cannot take any more.

Acknowledgements

Acknowledgements are due to the editors of the following publications where some of these poems first appeared: *PN Review, Poetry Wales, Scintilla, Poetry Review, New Welsh Review, Planet.*